MW00714679

The do-it-yourself Guide to... Enjoying Retirement

by
Marianne Richmond

The do-it-yourself Guide to...
Enjoying Retirement

Marianne Richmond Studios, Inc.
3900 Stinson Boulevard NE
Minneapolis, MN 55421
www.mariannerichmond.com

ISBN 10: 1-934082-23-6
ISBN 13: 978-1-934082-23-2

Text by Marianne Richmond & Colleen Niznik
Illustrations by Marianne Richmond
Book design by Sara Dare Biscan

Printed in China

First Printing

TO

FROM

Date

Ahhhhhh, retirement — it's the
weekend that never ends!

Lest you're worried your extra free
time means a perpetual game of
solitaire, we have created just for
you the do-it-yourself Guide
to Enjoying your Retirement.

This handy guide will jump-start your brain into realizing all the ways you can enjoy your newfound freedom.

Congratulations
— it's time to par-tay!

Enough said.

Indulge your Creativity.

Take up a new hobby —
seed portraiture, watermelon
sculpting, or making figurines out of
hardware. You'll never need to go
last-minute holiday shopping again!

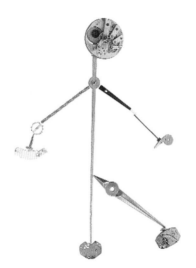

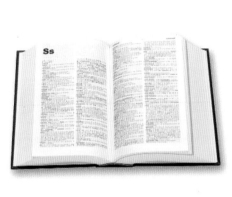

Revamp your vocabulary.

Lazy = Contemplative
Old = Knowledgeable
Aimless = Open to possibility
Boring = Appreciates the
simple things in life
Unscheduled = Spontaneous

Cultivate an Expertise.

Delve into the anatomy of
a seahorse or the origins of
synchronized swimming. Your
new knowledge will be a boon
to uninspiring dinner parties and
limit your use of the phrase,
"back in my day..."

first trunk ring

pectoral fin

superior
trunk ridge

lateral
trunk ridge

keel

inferior trunk ridge

dorsal fin

last trunk ring

anal fin

first tail ring

Resist the urge to
retire your common sense.

Think twice about dying your hair,
getting plastic surgery or buying
those "trendy" clothes at the mall.
While you may not need to
impress the boss or clients — first
impressions still count for something

(an invitation to complete a foursome

at the golf course, perhaps!).

Start any day with a game of "random roam."

Rules:

Pour cup of coffee. Open a map. Close your eyes and point to a location. Drive there and explore (Winnebago optional).

This will certainly eject you from your comfort zone — and away from the leaky faucet you've been meaning to fix.

Celebrate your seniority ...

Compile a list of places about town that offer senior discounts. Resist the urge, however, to go out for 56¢ burgers every day — your heart will seek revenge.

And indulge your kid at heart.

Go ahead... get that
convertible! Be sure to drive
by as many teenage boys
as possible to watch them
drool over your "ride".

Keep a hush on the hush-hush.

In other words: Keep past
transgressions in the past.

Now is not the time to come clean about harmless office flirtations, over-the-top holiday parties or how you were the one who took the boss's lunch from the fridge. Many of your friends are still within earshot of people who still care.

Stay on this side of the deep end.

Reject the desire to use a highly decorated golf cart as your preferred mode of transportation. Though you may wish to merrily putt along, you may inspire unprecedented levels of name calling and profanity from trailing motorists.

Consider a part-time
influx of cash.

With no fear of being fired, you
can be the free-spirited employee
who baffles all. Get a job that
offers large discounts on your
wish-list "toys." Plasma TV or
vibrating recliner at 40% off?

You're there!

Re-friend somebody.

Remember that pal from years ago?
The one you haven't spoke with since
your fraternity days in college?
Look him or her up. Then go visit!
If nothing else, you'll enjoy a free
tour guide and, hopefully, lodging.

Re-activate.

Join a slow-pitch softball team or bowling league. Call yourselves the **"radical retirees"** and wear tie-dye uniforms. This is the only excuse you'll ever have to wear tie-dye anything. Even if you need to fake your way through the sports part, there is always a trip to the bar afterwards!

Don't be a "pain on the block."

With additional time to putter, walk away from any desire to paint your house cotton candy pink, win the Christmas lights competition, or parade your set of plastic pink flamingoes across the lawn. And please — don't start giving away toothbrushes for Halloween.

Loan yourself out.

Sub for a sick politician during summer parades. Offer to be a fill-in grandparent for local schools and day cares centers. Or be an on-call Bingo caller or Auctioneer.

Shush the medical matters.

While attending a Mexican Fiesta, you may feel like everyone is wondering why you aren't eating the "inferno chimichangas."

They aren't wondering, so don't try to explain by talking about the intricacies of your colon.

Lastly ...

Live it up!

You worked for five decades (give or take a couple years to re-find yourself) to get to this point! Life goes by too quickly

to spend it $\overset{\text{all}}{\wedge}$ sleeping in. You have
a lot of living to do, things to
accomplish, hobbies to learn, people
and places to see...

Hmmm... Maybe you'll need to
buy a new alarm clock
after all, so you won't miss out
on your new adventures!

Congratulations on your retirement!

A gifted author and artist, Marianne Richmond shares her creations with millions of people worldwide through her delightful books, cards, and giftware.

To learn more about Marianne's products, please visit www.mariannerichmond.com.